SHIP'S LOG

MEHITABEL
MAHITABEL

Vessel Name

This Book Covers The Period

OCT. 2014 to _____
Starting   Ending

Copyright © 2003 by John Kokulis

Library of Congress Number: 2003096683
ISBN :   Hardcover   1-4134-3098-8
           Softcover   1-4134-3097-X

All rights reserved. No part of this book may be reproduced or transmitted in any form or by any means, electronic or mechanical, including photocopying, recording, or by any information storage and retrieval system, without permission in writing from the copyright owner.

This book was printed in the United States of America.

To order additional copies of this book, contact:
Xlibris Corporation
1-888-795-4274
www.Xlibris.com
Orders@Xlibris.com

To the ultimate "crew":

my wife Terri,

daughter Stephanie,

and

son Alexander

SHIP'S LOG

TABLE OF CONTENTS

Boat Information 1
Daily Log 3
Maintenance Log 65
Fuel Log 85
Equipment Log 91
    Bulbs 97
    Fuses 99
Sail Inventory 101
Radio/VHF Log 105
Wine Log 111
Restaurant Log 119
"Watering-Hole" Log 127
Marine Log 133
Fish Log 139
GPS Log 147
Notes 155

Boat Information

MAKE & YEAR: _____

MODEL NAME: _____

VESSEL NAME*: _____

HAILING PORT*: _____

HULL ID #: _____

REGISTRATION #: _____

INSURANCE COMPANY & POLICY #: _____

INSURANCE AGENT & TELEPHONE #: _____

BOAT DIMENSIONS:
- Length Overall (LOA): _____
- Beam: _____
- Draft: _____

YACHT YARD INFORMATION:
- Boat docked at: _____
- Address: _____
  _____
- Key Contact: _____
- Phone #: _____
- Email Address: _____

Boat Information - continued

Fuel Type: _____

Fuel Tank Capacity -   Left/Single: _____
                        Right: _____

Fuel Filter Type: _____

Replace Filter Every: _____ engine hours

Engine Oil Type: _____

Change Engine Oil Every: _____ engine hours

Engine Oil Filter Type: _____

Change Oil Filter Every: _____ engine hours

Other Rountine Maintenance Activity - 1: _____
_____

Perform Task Every: _____ engine hours

Other Routine Maintenance Activity - 2: _____
_____

Perform Task Every: _____ engine hours

Other Routine Maintenance Activity - 3: _____
_____

Perform Task Every: _____ engine hours

Tel # Of Maintenance Dept of Boat Mfg: _____
Email Of Maintenance Dept of Boat Mfg: _____

DAILY LOG

DAILY LOG

Date:	Departing From:	Estimated Arrival Time:
Engine Hours:	Destination Port:	Actual Arrival Time:

Weather Conditions:

  Wind:

  Seas:

  Waves:

On Board Today

The "Regulars":　　Our "Guests":

_____　_____

_____　_____

_____　_____

_____　_____

Skipper's Comments: _____

_____
_____
_____
_____
_____
_____
_____
_____
_____
_____
_____
_____
_____
_____
_____
_____
_____

DAILY LOG
continued

Skipper's Comments (continued): _____

Guest Comments: (Remember, these comments will be taken into account when the Skipper considers further invitations for you to come aboard)

DAILY LOG

Date:	Departing From:	Estimated Arrival Time:
Engine Hours:	Destination Port:	Actual Arrival Time:

Weather Conditions:

　　Wind:

　　Seas:

　　Waves:

On Board Today

The "Regulars":	Our "Guests":
_____	_____
_____	_____
_____	_____
_____	_____

Skipper's Comments: _____

_____

_____

_____

_____

_____

_____

_____

_____

_____

_____

_____

_____

_____

DAILY LOG
continued

Skipper's Comments (continued): _____

_____
_____
_____
_____
_____
_____
_____
_____
_____
_____
_____
_____

Guest Comments: (Remember, these comments will be taken into account when the Skipper considers further invitations for you to come aboard)

_____
_____
_____
_____
_____
_____
_____
_____
_____
_____
_____
_____
_____
_____
_____
_____
_____
_____

DAILY LOG

Date:	Departing From:	Estimated Arrival Time:
Engine Hours:	Destination Port:	Actual Arrival Time:

Weather Conditions:

   Wind:

   Seas:

   Waves:

On Board Today

The "Regulars":	Our "Guests":
_____	_____
_____	_____
_____	_____
_____	_____

Skipper's Comments: _____

_____
_____
_____
_____
_____
_____
_____
_____
_____
_____
_____
_____
_____
_____

DAILY LOG
continued

Skipper's Comments (continued): _____

_____
_____
_____
_____
_____
_____
_____
_____
_____
_____
_____

Guest Comments: (Remember, these comments will be taken into account when the Skipper considers further invitations for you to come aboard)

_____
_____
_____
_____
_____
_____
_____
_____
_____
_____
_____
_____
_____
_____
_____
_____
_____
_____

DAILY LOG

Date:	Departing From:	Estimated Arrival Time:
Engine Hours:	Destination Port:	Actual Arrival Time:

Weather Conditions:

　Wind:

　Seas:

　Waves:

On Board Today

The "Regulars":　　Our "Guests":

_____　_____

_____　_____

_____　_____

_____　_____

Skipper's
Comments: _____

_____

_____

_____

_____

_____

_____

_____

_____

_____

_____

_____

_____

_____

DAILY LOG
continued

Skipper's Comments (continued): _____

_____
_____
_____
_____
_____
_____
_____
_____
_____
_____
_____

Guest Comments: (Remember, these comments will be taken into account when the Skipper considers further invitations for you to come aboard)

_____
_____
_____
_____
_____
_____
_____
_____
_____
_____
_____
_____
_____
_____
_____
_____
_____
_____
_____

DAILY LOG

Date:	Departing From:	Estimated Arrival Time:
Engine Hours:	Destination Port:	Actual Arrival Time:

Weather Conditions:	On Board Today	
	The "Regulars":	Our "Guests":
Wind:	_____	_____
	_____	_____
Seas:	_____	_____
	_____	_____
Waves:	_____	_____
	_____	_____

Skipper's
Comments: _____

_____
_____
_____
_____
_____
_____
_____
_____
_____
_____
_____
_____
_____
_____
_____

DAILY LOG
continued

Skipper's Comments (continued): _____

_____
_____
_____
_____
_____
_____
_____
_____
_____
_____
_____
_____

Guest Comments: (Remember, these comments will be taken into account when the Skipper considers further invitations for you to come aboard)

_____
_____
_____
_____
_____
_____
_____
_____
_____
_____
_____
_____
_____
_____
_____
_____
_____
_____
_____
_____
_____

DAILY LOG

Date:	Departing From:	Estimated Arrival Time:
Engine Hours:	Destination Port:	Actual Arrival Time:

Weather Conditions:

   Wind:

   Seas:

   Waves:

On Board Today

The "Regulars":   Our "Guests":

_____ _____

_____ _____

_____ _____

_____ _____

Skipper's Comments: _____

_____
_____
_____
_____
_____
_____
_____
_____
_____
_____
_____
_____
_____
_____
_____

DAILY LOG
continued

Skipper's Comments (continued): _____

_____
_____
_____
_____
_____
_____
_____
_____
_____
_____
_____
_____

Guest Comments: (Remember, these comments will be taken into account when the Skipper considers further invitations for you to come aboard)

_____
_____
_____
_____
_____
_____
_____
_____
_____
_____
_____
_____
_____
_____
_____
_____
_____
_____

DAILY LOG

Date:	Departing From:	Estimated Arrival Time:
Engine Hours:	Destination Port:	Actual Arrival Time:

Weather Conditions:

Wind:

Seas:

Waves:

On Board Today

The "Regulars":   Our "Guests":

_____   _____
_____   _____
_____   _____
_____   _____

Skipper's
Comments: _____

_____
_____
_____
_____
_____
_____
_____
_____
_____
_____
_____
_____
_____
_____
_____

DAILY LOG
continued

Skipper's Comments (continued): _____

_____
_____
_____
_____
_____
_____
_____
_____
_____
_____
_____
_____

Guest Comments: (Remember, these comments will be taken into account when the Skipper considers further invitations for you to come aboard)

_____
_____
_____
_____
_____
_____
_____
_____
_____
_____
_____
_____
_____
_____
_____
_____
_____
_____
_____

DAILY LOG

Date:	Departing From:	Estimated Arrival Time:
Engine Hours:	Destination Port:	Actual Arrival Time:

Weather Conditions:

   Wind:

   Seas:

   Waves:

On Board Today

The "Regulars":　　Our "Guests":

_____　_____

_____　_____

_____　_____

_____　_____

Skipper's Comments: _____

_____

_____

_____

_____

_____

_____

_____

_____

_____

_____

_____

DAILY LOG
continued

Skipper's Comments (continued): _____
_____
_____
_____
_____
_____
_____
_____
_____
_____
_____
_____
_____

Guest Comments: <u>(Remember, these comments will be taken into account when the Skipper considers further invitations for you to come aboard)</u>
_____
_____
_____
_____
_____
_____
_____
_____
_____
_____
_____
_____
_____
_____
_____
_____
_____
_____
_____
_____

DAILY LOG

Date:	Departing From:	Estimated Arrival Time:
Engine Hours:	Destination Port:	Actual Arrival Time:

Weather Conditions:

   Wind:

   Seas:

   Waves:

On Board Today

The "Regulars":   Our "Guests":

_____ _____

_____ _____

_____ _____

_____ _____

Skipper's Comments: _____

_____
_____
_____
_____
_____
_____
_____
_____
_____
_____
_____
_____
_____
_____
_____
_____

DAILY LOG
continued

Skipper's Comments (continued): _____

_____
_____
_____
_____
_____
_____
_____
_____
_____
_____
_____
_____

Guest Comments: (Remember, these comments will be taken into account when the Skipper considers further invitations for you to come aboard)

_____
_____
_____
_____
_____
_____
_____
_____
_____
_____
_____
_____
_____
_____
_____
_____
_____
_____
_____
_____

DAILY LOG

Date:	Departing From:	Estimated Arrival Time:
Engine Hours:	Destination Port:	Actual Arrival Time:

Weather Conditions:　　　　　　　　　　On Board Today

　　　　　　　　　　　　　　The "Regulars":　　Our "Guests":

　Wind:　　　　　　　　　　　_____　_____

　Seas:　　　　　　　　　　　_____　_____

　Waves:　　　　　　　　　　_____　_____

　　　　　　　　　　　　　　_____　_____

Skipper's
Comments: _____

_____
_____
_____
_____
_____
_____
_____
_____
_____
_____
_____
_____
_____
_____
_____

DAILY LOG
continued

Skipper's Comments (continued): _____

_____
_____
_____
_____
_____
_____
_____
_____
_____
_____
_____

Guest Comments: (Remember, these comments will be taken into account when the Skipper considers further invitations for you to come aboard)

_____
_____
_____
_____
_____
_____
_____
_____
_____
_____
_____
_____
_____
_____
_____
_____
_____
_____
_____

DAILY LOG

Date:	Departing From:	Estimated Arrival Time:
Engine Hours:	Destination Port:	Actual Arrival Time:

Weather Conditions:

   Wind:

   Seas:

   Waves:

On Board Today

The "Regulars":	Our "Guests":
_____	_____
_____	_____
_____	_____
_____	_____

Skipper's Comments: _____

_____

_____

_____

_____

_____

_____

_____

_____

_____

_____

_____

_____

_____

_____

DAILY LOG
continued

Skipper's Comments (continued): _____

_____
_____
_____
_____
_____
_____
_____
_____
_____
_____
_____
_____

Guest Comments: (Remember, these comments will be taken into account when the Skipper considers further invitations for you to come aboard)

_____
_____
_____
_____
_____
_____
_____
_____
_____
_____
_____
_____
_____
_____
_____
_____
_____
_____

DAILY LOG

Date:	Departing From:	Estimated Arrival Time:
Engine Hours:	Destination Port:	Actual Arrival Time:

Weather Conditions:	On Board Today
Wind: Seas: Waves:	The "Regulars": Our "Guests": _____ _____ _____ _____ _____ _____ _____ _____

Skipper's
Comments: _____

_____
_____
_____
_____
_____
_____
_____
_____
_____
_____
_____
_____
_____
_____
_____

DAILY LOG
continued

Skipper's Comments (continued): _____

_____
_____
_____
_____
_____
_____
_____
_____
_____
_____
_____
_____

Guest Comments: (Remember, these comments will be taken into account when the Skipper considers further invitations for you to come aboard)

_____
_____
_____
_____
_____
_____
_____
_____
_____
_____
_____
_____
_____
_____
_____
_____
_____
_____

DAILY LOG

Date:	Departing From:	Estimated Arrival Time:
Engine Hours:	Destination Port:	Actual Arrival Time:

Weather Conditions:

   Wind:

   Seas:

   Waves:

On Board Today

The "Regulars":	Our "Guests":
_____	_____
_____	_____
_____	_____
_____	_____

Skipper's Comments: _____
_____
_____
_____
_____
_____
_____
_____
_____
_____
_____
_____
_____
_____
_____
_____
_____

DAILY LOG
continued

Skipper's Comments (continued): _____

_____
_____
_____
_____
_____
_____
_____
_____
_____
_____
_____
_____

Guest Comments: (Remember, these comments will be taken into account when the Skipper considers further invitations for you to come aboard)

_____
_____
_____
_____
_____
_____
_____
_____
_____
_____
_____
_____
_____
_____
_____
_____
_____
_____

DAILY LOG

Date:	Departing From:	Estimated Arrival Time:
Engine Hours:	Destination Port:	Actual Arrival Time:

Weather Conditions:	On Board Today	
	The "Regulars":	Our "Guests":
Wind:	_____	_____
	_____	_____
Seas:	_____	_____
	_____	_____
Waves:	_____	_____
	_____	_____

Skipper's
Comments: _____
_____
_____
_____
_____
_____
_____
_____
_____
_____
_____
_____
_____
_____
_____

DAILY LOG
continued

Skipper's Comments (continued): _____

_____
_____
_____
_____
_____
_____
_____
_____
_____
_____
_____
_____

Guest Comments: (Remember, these comments will be taken into account when the Skipper considers further invitations for you to come aboard)

_____
_____
_____
_____
_____
_____
_____
_____
_____
_____
_____
_____
_____
_____
_____
_____
_____
_____
_____

DAILY LOG

Date:	Departing From:	Estimated Arrival Time:
Engine Hours:	Destination Port:	Actual Arrival Time:

Weather Conditions: Wind: Seas: Waves:	On Board Today The "Regulars": Our "Guests": _____ _____ _____ _____ _____ _____ _____ _____

Skipper's
Comments: _____

_____
_____
_____
_____
_____
_____
_____
_____
_____
_____
_____
_____
_____
_____

DAILY LOG
continued

Skipper's Comments (continued): _____

_____
_____
_____
_____
_____
_____
_____
_____
_____
_____
_____

Guest Comments: (Remember, these comments will be taken into account when the Skipper considers further invitations for you to come aboard)

_____
_____
_____
_____
_____
_____
_____
_____
_____
_____
_____
_____
_____
_____
_____
_____
_____
_____
_____

DAILY LOG

Date:	Departing From:	Estimated Arrival Time:
Engine Hours:	Destination Port:	Actual Arrival Time:

| Weather Conditions:

  Wind:

  Seas:

  Waves: | On Board Today
The "Regulars": Our "Guests":
_____ _____
_____ _____
_____ _____
_____ _____ |

Skipper's
Comments: _____

_____
_____
_____
_____
_____
_____
_____
_____
_____
_____
_____
_____
_____
_____

DAILY LOG
continued

Skipper's Comments (continued): _____

Guest Comments: (Remember, these comments will be taken into account when the Skipper considers further invitations for you to come aboard)

DAILY LOG

Date:	Departing From:	Estimated Arrival Time:
Engine Hours:	Destination Port:	Actual Arrival Time:

Weather Conditions:

   Wind:

   Seas:

   Waves:

On Board Today

The "Regulars":   Our "Guests":

_____ _____

_____ _____

_____ _____

_____ _____

Skipper's
Comments: _____

_____

_____

_____

_____

_____

_____

_____

_____

_____

_____

_____

_____

_____

DAILY LOG
continued

Skipper's Comments (continued): _____

_____
_____
_____
_____
_____
_____
_____
_____
_____
_____

Guest Comments: (Remember, these comments will be taken into account when the Skipper considers further invitations for you to come aboard)

_____
_____
_____
_____
_____
_____
_____
_____
_____
_____
_____
_____
_____
_____
_____
_____
_____
_____

DAILY LOG

Date:	Departing From:	Estimated Arrival Time:
Engine Hours:	Destination Port:	Actual Arrival Time:

Weather Conditions:

   Wind:

   Seas:

   Waves:

On Board Today

The "Regulars":   Our "Guests":

_____ _____

_____ _____

_____ _____

_____ _____

Skipper's Comments: _____

_____
_____
_____
_____
_____
_____
_____
_____
_____
_____
_____
_____
_____
_____
_____
_____

DAILY LOG
continued

Skipper's Comments (continued): _____

_____
_____
_____
_____
_____
_____
_____
_____
_____
_____
_____
_____

Guest Comments: (Remember, these comments will be taken into account when the Skipper considers further invitations for you to come aboard)

_____
_____
_____
_____
_____
_____
_____
_____
_____
_____
_____
_____
_____
_____
_____
_____
_____
_____
_____
_____
_____

DAILY LOG

Date:	Departing From:	Estimated Arrival Time:
Engine Hours:	Destination Port:	Actual Arrival Time:

Weather Conditions:

   Wind:

   Seas:

   Waves:

On Board Today

The "Regulars":   Our "Guests":

_____ _____

_____ _____

_____ _____

_____ _____

Skipper's
Comments: _____

_____

_____

_____

_____

_____

_____

_____

_____

_____

_____

_____

_____

_____

_____

_____

DAILY LOG
continued

Skipper's Comments (continued): _____

_____
_____
_____
_____
_____
_____
_____
_____
_____
_____
_____
_____

Guest Comments: (Remember, these comments will be taken into account when the Skipper considers further invitations for you to come aboard)

_____
_____
_____
_____
_____
_____
_____
_____
_____
_____
_____
_____
_____
_____
_____
_____
_____
_____

DAILY LOG

Date:	Departing From:	Estimated Arrival Time:
Engine Hours:	Destination Port:	Actual Arrival Time:

Weather Conditions:

   Wind:

   Seas:

   Waves:

On Board Today

The "Regulars":   Our "Guests":

_____ _____

_____ _____

_____ _____

_____ _____

Skipper's
Comments: _____

_____

_____

_____

_____

_____

_____

_____

_____

_____

_____

_____

_____

DAILY LOG
continued

Skipper's Comments (continued): _____

_____
_____
_____
_____
_____
_____
_____
_____
_____
_____
_____
_____

Guest Comments: (Remember, these comments will be taken into account when the Skipper considers further invitations for you to come aboard)

_____
_____
_____
_____
_____
_____
_____
_____
_____
_____
_____
_____
_____
_____
_____
_____
_____

DAILY LOG

Date:	Departing From:	Estimated Arrival Time:
Engine Hours:	Destination Port:	Actual Arrival Time:

Weather Conditions:

   Wind:

   Seas:

   Waves:

On Board Today

The "Regulars":   Our "Guests":

_____ _____

_____ _____

_____ _____

_____ _____

Skipper's
Comments: _____
_____
_____
_____
_____
_____
_____
_____
_____
_____
_____
_____
_____
_____
_____
_____
_____

DAILY LOG
continued

Skipper's Comments (continued): _____

_____
_____
_____
_____
_____
_____
_____
_____
_____
_____
_____

Guest Comments: (Remember, these comments will be taken into account when the Skipper considers further invitations for you to come aboard)

_____
_____
_____
_____
_____
_____
_____
_____
_____
_____
_____
_____
_____
_____
_____
_____
_____
_____

DAILY LOG

Date:	Departing From:	Estimated Arrival Time:
Engine Hours:	Destination Port:	Actual Arrival Time:

Weather Conditions:　　　　　　　　　　On Board Today

　　　　　　　　　　　　　　　　The "Regulars":　　Our "Guests":

　Wind:　　　　　　　　　　　_____　_____

　Seas:　　　　　　　　　　　_____　_____

　Waves:　　　　　　　　　　_____　_____

　　　　　　　　　　　　　　　_____　_____

Skipper's
Comments: _____
_____
_____
_____
_____
_____
_____
_____
_____
_____
_____
_____
_____
_____
_____
_____

DAILY LOG
continued

Skipper's Comments (continued): _____

_____
_____
_____
_____
_____
_____
_____
_____
_____
_____
_____

Guest Comments: (Remember, these comments will be taken into account when the Skipper considers further invitations for you to come aboard)

_____
_____
_____
_____
_____
_____
_____
_____
_____
_____
_____
_____
_____
_____
_____
_____
_____
_____
_____

DAILY LOG

Date:	Departing From:	Estimated Arrival Time:
Engine Hours:	Destination Port:	Actual Arrival Time:

Weather Conditions:
 	
  Wind:
 	
  Seas:
 	
  Waves:
	On Board Today
	The "Regulars": Our "Guests":
	_____ _____
	_____ _____
	_____ _____
	_____ _____

Skipper's
Comments: _____
_____
_____
_____
_____
_____
_____
_____
_____
_____
_____
_____
_____
_____

DAILY LOG
continued

Skipper's Comments (continued): _____

_____
_____
_____
_____
_____
_____
_____
_____
_____
_____
_____
_____

Guest Comments: (Remember, these comments will be taken into account when the Skipper considers further invitations for you to come aboard)

_____
_____
_____
_____
_____
_____
_____
_____
_____
_____
_____
_____
_____
_____
_____
_____
_____
_____
_____
_____

DAILY LOG

Date:	Departing From:	Estimated Arrival Time:
Engine Hours:	Destination Port:	Actual Arrival Time:

Weather Conditions:	On Board Today	
	The "Regulars":	Our "Guests":
Wind:	_____	_____
Seas:	_____	_____
Waves:	_____	_____
	_____	_____

Skipper's Comments: _____
_____
_____
_____
_____
_____
_____
_____
_____
_____
_____
_____
_____
_____
_____
_____

DAILY LOG
continued

Skipper's Comments (continued): _____

_____
_____
_____
_____
_____
_____
_____
_____
_____
_____
_____

Guest Comments: (Remember, these comments will be taken into account when the Skipper considers further invitations for you to come aboard)

_____
_____
_____
_____
_____
_____
_____
_____
_____
_____
_____
_____
_____
_____
_____
_____
_____

DAILY LOG

Date:	Departing From:	Estimated Arrival Time:
Engine Hours:	Destination Port:	Actual Arrival Time:

Weather Conditions:

Wind:

Seas:

Waves:

On Board Today

The "Regulars":   Our "Guests":

_____   _____

_____   _____

_____   _____

_____   _____

Skipper's Comments: _____

_____

_____

_____

_____

_____

_____

_____

_____

_____

_____

_____

_____

_____

DAILY LOG
continued

Skipper's Comments (continued): _____

_____
_____
_____
_____
_____
_____
_____
_____
_____
_____
_____
_____

Guest Comments: (Remember, these comments will be taken into account when the Skipper considers further invitations for you to come aboard)

_____
_____
_____
_____
_____
_____
_____
_____
_____
_____
_____
_____
_____
_____
_____
_____
_____
_____

DAILY LOG

Date:	Departing From:	Estimated Arrival Time:
Engine Hours:	Destination Port:	Actual Arrival Time:

Weather Conditions:

   Wind:

   Seas:

   Waves:

On Board Today

The "Regulars":	Our "Guests":
_____	_____
_____	_____
_____	_____
_____	_____

Skipper's Comments: _____

_____

_____

_____

_____

_____

_____

_____

_____

_____

_____

_____

_____

_____

DAILY LOG
continued

Skipper's Comments (continued): _____

_____
_____
_____
_____
_____
_____
_____
_____
_____
_____
_____

Guest Comments: (Remember, these comments will be taken into account when the Skipper considers further invitations for you to come aboard)

_____
_____
_____
_____
_____
_____
_____
_____
_____
_____
_____
_____
_____
_____
_____
_____
_____
_____

DAILY LOG

Date:	Departing From:	Estimated Arrival Time:
Engine Hours:	Destination Port:	Actual Arrival Time:

Weather Conditions:

   Wind:

   Seas:

   Waves:

On Board Today

The "Regulars":   Our "Guests":

_____ _____

_____ _____

_____ _____

_____ _____

Skipper's Comments: _____

_____
_____
_____
_____
_____
_____
_____
_____
_____
_____
_____
_____
_____
_____
_____
_____

DAILY LOG
continued

Skipper's Comments (continued): _____

_____
_____
_____
_____
_____
_____
_____
_____
_____
_____
_____
_____

Guest Comments: (Remember, these comments will be taken into account when the Skipper considers further invitations for you to come aboard)

_____
_____
_____
_____
_____
_____
_____
_____
_____
_____
_____
_____
_____
_____
_____
_____
_____
_____
_____

DAILY LOG

Date:	Departing From:	Estimated Arrival Time:
Engine Hours:	Destination Port:	Actual Arrival Time:

Weather Conditions:

   Wind:

   Seas:

   Waves:

On Board Today

The "Regulars":   Our "Guests":

_____ _____

_____ _____

_____ _____

_____ _____

Skipper's Comments: _____

_____

_____

_____

_____

_____

_____

_____

_____

_____

_____

_____

_____

_____

_____

DAILY LOG
continued

Skipper's Comments (continued): _____

_____
_____
_____
_____
_____
_____
_____
_____
_____
_____
_____
_____

Guest Comments: (Remember, these comments will be taken into account when the Skipper considers further invitations for you to come aboard)

_____
_____
_____
_____
_____
_____
_____
_____
_____
_____
_____
_____
_____
_____
_____
_____
_____
_____

DAILY LOG

Date:	Departing From:	Estimated Arrival Time:
Engine Hours:	Destination Port:	Actual Arrival Time:

Weather Conditions:

   Wind:

   Seas:

   Waves:

On Board Today

The "Regulars":   Our "Guests":

_____ _____

_____ _____

_____ _____

_____ _____

Skipper's
Comments: _____

_____

_____

_____

_____

_____

_____

_____

_____

_____

_____

_____

_____

_____

_____

_____

DAILY LOG
continued

Skipper's Comments (continued): _____

_____
_____
_____
_____
_____
_____
_____
_____
_____
_____
_____
_____

Guest Comments: (Remember, these comments will be taken into account when the Skipper considers further invitations for you to come aboard)

_____
_____
_____
_____
_____
_____
_____
_____
_____
_____
_____
_____
_____
_____
_____
_____
_____
_____

MAINTENANCE LOG

Maintenance Log

Date: _____ ☐ Scheduled ☐ Unscheduled
Engine Hours: _____

Description of Problem: _____
_____
_____
_____

Maintenance Performed By: _____

Corrective Actions: _____
_____
_____
_____

Total Repair Costs: _____

Date: _____ ☐ Scheduled ☐ Unscheduled
Engine Hours: _____

Description of Problem: _____
_____
_____
_____

Maintenance Performed By: _____

Corrective Actions: _____
_____
_____
_____

Total Repair Costs: _____

Maintenance Log

Date: _____ ☐ Scheduled ☐ Unscheduled
Engine Hours: _____

Description of Problem: _____
_____
_____
_____
_____

Maintenance Performed By: _____

Corrective Actions: _____
_____
_____
_____
_____

Total Repair Costs: _____

Date: _____ ☐ Scheduled ☐ Unscheduled
Engine Hours: _____

Description of Problem: _____
_____
_____
_____
_____

Maintenance Performed By: _____

Corrective Actions: _____
_____
_____
_____
_____

Total Repair Costs: _____

Maintenance Log

Date: _____ ☐ Scheduled   ☐ Unscheduled
Engine Hours: _____

Description of Problem: _____
_____
_____
_____
_____

Maintenance Performed By: _____

Corrective Actions: _____
_____
_____
_____
_____

Total Repair Costs: _____

Date: _____ ☐ Scheduled   ☐ Unscheduled
Engine Hours: _____

Description of Problem: _____
_____
_____
_____
_____

Maintenance Performed By: _____

Corrective Actions: _____
_____
_____
_____
_____

Total Repair Costs: _____

Maintenance Log

Date: _____ ☐ Scheduled ☐ Unscheduled
Engine Hours: _____

Description of Problem: _____
_____
_____
_____
_____

Maintenance Performed By: _____

Corrective Actions: _____
_____
_____
_____
_____

Total Repair Costs: _____

Date: _____ ☐ Scheduled ☐ Unscheduled
Engine Hours: _____

Description of Problem: _____
_____
_____
_____
_____

Maintenance Performed By: _____

Corrective Actions: _____
_____
_____
_____
_____

Total Repair Costs: _____

Maintenance Log

Date: _____ ☐ Scheduled ☐ Unscheduled
Engine Hours: _____

Description of Problem: _____
_____
_____
_____
_____

Maintenance Performed By: _____

Corrective Actions: _____
_____
_____
_____
_____

Total Repair Costs: _____

Date: _____ ☐ Scheduled ☐ Unscheduled
Engine Hours: _____

Description of Problem: _____
_____
_____
_____
_____

Maintenance Performed By: _____

Corrective Actions: _____
_____
_____
_____
_____

Total Repair Costs: _____

Maintenance Log

Date: _____ ☐ Scheduled ☐ Unscheduled
Engine Hours: _____

Description of Problem: _____
_____
_____
_____
_____

Maintenance Performed By: _____

Corrective Actions: _____
_____
_____
_____
_____

Total Repair Costs: _____

Date: _____ ☐ Scheduled ☐ Unscheduled
Engine Hours: _____

Description of Problem: _____
_____
_____
_____
_____

Maintenance Performed By: _____

Corrective Actions: _____
_____
_____
_____
_____

Total Repair Costs: _____

Maintenance Log

Date: _____ ☐ Scheduled ☐ Unscheduled
Engine Hours: _____

Description of Problem: _____
_____
_____
_____
_____

Maintenance Performed By: _____

Corrective Actions: _____
_____
_____
_____
_____

Total Repair Costs: _____

Date: _____ ☐ Scheduled ☐ Unscheduled
Engine Hours: _____

Description of Problem: _____
_____
_____
_____
_____

Maintenance Performed By: _____

Corrective Actions: _____
_____
_____
_____
_____

Total Repair Costs: _____

Maintenance Log

Date: _____ ☐ Scheduled ☐ Unscheduled
Engine Hours: _____

Description of Problem: _____
_____
_____
_____
_____

Maintenance Performed By: _____

Corrective Actions: _____
_____
_____
_____
_____

Total Repair Costs: _____

Date: _____ ☐ Scheduled ☐ Unscheduled
Engine Hours: _____

Description of Problem: _____
_____
_____
_____
_____

Maintenance Performed By: _____

Corrective Actions: _____
_____
_____
_____
_____

Total Repair Costs: _____

Maintenance Log

Date: _____ ☐ Scheduled ☐ Unscheduled
Engine Hours: _____

Description of Problem: _____
_____
_____
_____
_____

Maintenance Performed By: _____

Corrective Actions: _____
_____
_____
_____
_____

Total Repair Costs: _____

Date: _____ ☐ Scheduled ☐ Unscheduled
Engine Hours: _____

Description of Problem: _____
_____
_____
_____
_____

Maintenance Performed By: _____

Corrective Actions: _____
_____
_____
_____
_____

Total Repair Costs: _____

Maintenance Log

Date: _____ ☐ Scheduled ☐ Unscheduled
Engine Hours: _____

Description of Problem: _____
_____
_____
_____
_____

Maintenance Performed By: _____

Corrective Actions: _____
_____
_____
_____
_____

Total Repair Costs: _____

Date: _____ ☐ Scheduled ☐ Unscheduled
Engine Hours: _____

Description of Problem: _____
_____
_____
_____
_____

Maintenance Performed By: _____

Corrective Actions: _____
_____
_____
_____
_____

Total Repair Costs: _____

Maintenance Log

Date: _____ ☐ Scheduled ☐ Unscheduled
Engine Hours: _____

Description of Problem: _____
_____
_____
_____
_____

Maintenance Performed By: _____

Corrective Actions: _____
_____
_____
_____
_____

Total Repair Costs: _____

Date: _____ ☐ Scheduled ☐ Unscheduled
Engine Hours: _____

Description of Problem: _____
_____
_____
_____
_____

Maintenance Performed By: _____

Corrective Actions: _____
_____
_____
_____
_____

Total Repair Costs: _____

Maintenance Log

Date: _____ ☐ Scheduled ☐ Unscheduled
Engine Hours: _____

Description of Problem: _____
_____
_____
_____
_____

Maintenance Performed By: _____

Corrective Actions: _____
_____
_____
_____
_____

Total Repair Costs: _____

Date: _____ ☐ Scheduled ☐ Unscheduled
Engine Hours: _____

Description of Problem: _____
_____
_____
_____
_____

Maintenance Performed By: _____

Corrective Actions: _____
_____
_____
_____
_____

Total Repair Costs: _____

Maintenance Log

Date: _____ ☐ Scheduled ☐ Unscheduled
Engine Hours: _____

Description of Problem: _____
_____
_____
_____
_____

Maintenance Performed By: _____

Corrective Actions: _____
_____
_____
_____
_____

Total Repair Costs: _____

Date: _____ ☐ Scheduled ☐ Unscheduled
Engine Hours: _____

Description of Problem: _____
_____
_____
_____
_____

Maintenance Performed By: _____

Corrective Actions: _____
_____
_____
_____
_____

Total Repair Costs: _____

Maintenance Log

Date: _____ ☐ Scheduled ☐ Unscheduled
Engine Hours: _____

Description of Problem: _____
_____
_____
_____
_____

Maintenance Performed By: _____

Corrective Actions: _____
_____
_____
_____
_____

Total Repair Costs: _____

Date: _____ ☐ Scheduled ☐ Unscheduled
Engine Hours: _____

Description of Problem: _____
_____
_____
_____
_____

Maintenance Performed By: _____

Corrective Actions: _____
_____
_____
_____
_____

Total Repair Costs: _____

Maintenance Log

Date: _____ ☐ Scheduled ☐ Unscheduled
Engine Hours: _____

Description of Problem: _____
_____
_____
_____
_____

Maintenance Performed By: _____

Corrective Actions: _____
_____
_____
_____
_____

Total Repair Costs: _____

Date: _____ ☐ Scheduled ☐ Unscheduled
Engine Hours: _____

Description of Problem: _____
_____
_____
_____
_____

Maintenance Performed By: _____

Corrective Actions: _____
_____
_____
_____
_____

Total Repair Costs: _____

Maintenance Log

Date: _____ ☐ Scheduled   ☐ Unscheduled
Engine Hours: _____

Description of Problem: _____
_____
_____
_____
_____

Maintenance Performed By: _____

Corrective Actions: _____
_____
_____
_____
_____

Total Repair Costs: _____

Date: _____ ☐ Scheduled   ☐ Unscheduled
Engine Hours: _____

Description of Problem: _____
_____
_____
_____
_____

Maintenance Performed By: _____

Corrective Actions: _____
_____
_____
_____
_____

Total Repair Costs: _____

Maintenance Log

Date: _____ ☐ Scheduled ☐ Unscheduled
Engine Hours: _____

Description of Problem: _____
_____
_____
_____
_____

Maintenance Performed By: _____

Corrective Actions: _____
_____
_____
_____
_____

Total Repair Costs: _____

Date: _____ ☐ Scheduled ☐ Unscheduled
Engine Hours: _____

Description of Problem: _____
_____
_____
_____
_____

Maintenance Performed By: _____

Corrective Actions: _____
_____
_____
_____
_____

Total Repair Costs: _____

Maintenance Log

Date: _____ ☐ Scheduled ☐ Unscheduled
Engine Hours: _____

Description of Problem: _____
_____
_____
_____
_____

Maintenance Performed By: _____

Corrective Actions: _____
_____
_____
_____
_____

Total Repair Costs: _____

Date: _____ ☐ Scheduled ☐ Unscheduled
Engine Hours: _____

Description of Problem: _____
_____
_____
_____
_____

Maintenance Performed By: _____

Corrective Actions: _____
_____
_____
_____
_____

Total Repair Costs: _____

FUEL LOG

FUEL LOG

Date	Engine Hours (Before Fill Up)	Gallons Added			Fueling Location	Cost Per Gallon	Gallons Per Engine Hour
		Left Tank	Right Tank	Total			

FUEL LOG

Date	Engine Hours (Before Fill Up)	Gallons Added			Fueling Location	Cost Per Gallon	Gallons Per Engine Hour
		Left Tank	Right Tank	Total			

FUEL LOG

Date	Engine Hours (Before Fill Up)	Gallons Added			Fueling Location	Cost Per Gallon	Gallons Per Engine Hour
		Left Tank	Right Tank	Total			

FUEL LOG

Date	Engine Hours (Before Fill Up)	Gallons Added			Fueling Location	Cost Per Gallon	Gallons Per Engine Hour
		Left Tank	Right Tank	Total			

FUEL LOG

Date	Engine Hours (Before Fill Up)	Gallons Added			Fueling Location	Cost Per Gallon	Gallons Per Engine Hour
		Left Tank	Right Tank	Total			

EQUIPMENT LOG

Equipment Log

Item 1: Engine - L   Make/Model _____
Serial #: _____   Manufacturer: _____
Comment: _____   Mfg/Contact Tel#: _____
_____   Mfg/Contact Email: _____

Item 2: Engine - R   Make/Model _____
Serial #: _____   Manufacturer: _____
Comment: _____   Mfg/Contact Tel#: _____
_____   Mfg/Contact Email: _____

Item 3: Battery (1/2/3)   Make/Model _____
Serial #: _____   Manufacturer: _____
Comment: _____   Mfg/Contact Tel#: _____
_____   Mfg/Contact Email: _____

Item 4: VHF   Make/Model _____
Serial #: _____   Manufacturer: _____
Comment: _____   Mfg/Contact Tel#: _____
_____   Mfg/Contact Email: _____

Item 5: GPS   Make/Model _____
Serial #: _____   Manufacturer: _____
Comment: _____   Mfg/Contact Tel#: _____
_____   Mfg/Contact Email: _____

Equipment Log

Item 6:   Chart plotter   Make/Model   _____
Serial #:   _____   Manufacturer: _____
Comment: _____   Mfg/Contact Tel#: _____
         _____   Mfg/Contact Email: _____

Item 7:   Fish finder   Make/Model   _____
Serial #:   _____   Manufacturer: _____
Comment: _____   Mfg/Contact Tel#: _____
         _____   Mfg/Contact Email: _____

Item 8:   Radar   Make/Model   _____
Serial #:   _____   Manufacturer: _____
Comment: _____   Mfg/Contact Tel#: _____
         _____   Mfg/Contact Email: _____

Item 9:   Radio/CD Player   Make/Model   _____
Serial #:   _____   Manufacturer: _____
Comment: _____   Mfg/Contact Tel#: _____
         _____   Mfg/Contact Email: _____

Item 10:   DVD Player/TV   Make/Model   _____
Serial #:   _____   Manufacturer: _____
Comment: _____   Mfg/Contact Tel#: _____
         _____   Mfg/Contact Email: _____

Equipment Log

Item 11: _____ Make/Model _____
Serial #: _____ Manufacturer: _____
Comment: _____ Mfg/Contact Tel#: _____
_____ Mfg/Contact Email: _____

Item 12: _____ Make/Model _____
Serial #: _____ Manufacturer: _____
Comment: _____ Mfg/Contact Tel#: _____
_____ Mfg/Contact Email: _____

Item 13: _____ Make/Model _____
Serial #: _____ Manufacturer: _____
Comment: _____ Mfg/Contact Tel#: _____
_____ Mfg/Contact Email: _____

Item 14: _____ Make/Model _____
Serial #: _____ Manufacturer: _____
Comment: _____ Mfg/Contact Tel#: _____
_____ Mfg/Contact Email: _____

Item 15: _____ Make/Model _____
Serial #: _____ Manufacturer: _____
Comment: _____ Mfg/Contact Tel#: _____
_____ Mfg/Contact Email: _____

Equipment Log

Item 16: _____   Make/Model   _____
Serial #: _____   Manufacturer: _____
Comment: _____   Mfg/Contact Tel#: _____
         _____   Mfg/Contact Email: _____

Item 17: _____   Make/Model   _____
Serial #: _____   Manufacturer: _____
Comment: _____   Mfg/Contact Tel#: _____
         _____   Mfg/Contact Email: _____

Item 18: _____   Make/Model   _____
Serial #: _____   Manufacturer: _____
Comment: _____   Mfg/Contact Tel#: _____
         _____   Mfg/Contact Email: _____

Item 19: _____   Make/Model   _____
Serial #: _____   Manufacturer: _____
Comment: _____   Mfg/Contact Tel#: _____
         _____   Mfg/Contact Email: _____

Item 20: _____   Make/Model   _____
Serial #: _____   Manufacturer: _____
Comment: _____   Mfg/Contact Tel#: _____
         _____   Mfg/Contact Email: _____

Equipment Log - continued

Bulbs: | Location | Bulb Type | Fuse |
| --- | --- | --- |
| | | |

Equipment Log - continued

Bulbs:　　　　Location　　　　Bulb Type　　　Fuse

Equipment Log - continued

Fuses:	For Equipment:	Location	Fuse Type

Equipment Log - continued

Fuses:	For Equipment:	Location	Fuse Type

SAIL INVENTORY

Sail Inventory

Sail Type / Description	Best Used Under Following Conditions
1.	
2.	
3.	
4.	
5.	
6.	

Sail Inventory

Sail Type / Description	Best Used Under Following Conditions
7.	
8.	
9.	
10.	
11.	
12.	

RADIO/VHF LOG

VHF Log

Channel	Description	Comment
16	Emergency	If your boat is in imminent danger and/or someone has been lost overboard, then send a distress call on Ch 16. Say "Mayday, Mayday, Mayday." Give your call sign and your boat name and location. Repeat until you receive an answer.
16	Calling Channel/ Monitoring Channel	If you which to establish communications with another station, then initiate call on Channel 16 and then, once contact is made, switch to another working Channel. When your VHF radio is turned on and not being used then you must monitor Channel 16
22	Coast Guard Channel	Use this channel to communicate with the Coast Guard (first make contact with them on Ch. 16).
6	Inter-ship Safety	Communicating navigational and weather warnings to other ships. For safety only.
WX1, WX2, WX3	Weather Channel	Continuous weather information from the NOAA (National Oceanic & Atmospheric Administration)
9, 68, 69, 71, 72, 78	Boat Operations (Non-Commercial)	For communications relating to your vessel and crew (i.e. rendezvous location, maneuvers, berthing, provisions, etc.)
24, 25, 26, 27, 28, 84, 85, 86, 87, 88	Marine Operator	For use to place a telephone call to any location in the world or to a vessel outside of your transmitting range. Contact the marine operator on assigned channel in your navigation area. If unknown, use Ch. 16

VHF Log

Channel	Description	Comment
15	Environmental	For use to receive broadcast information concerning the environmental conditions in which vessels operate: weather, sea conditions, time signals, notices to mariners, and hazards to navigation.
13	Navigation	For communications pertaining to the maneuvering of vessels or the directing of vessel movements. Commonly used by large vessels and tugboats
7,8,9, 10,11,18 19,67,79 80	Commercial	For use by commercial vessels
	Other:	
	Other:	
	Other:	
	Other:	

VHF Log

Channel	Description	Comment
	Other:	
	Other:	
	Other:	
	Other:	
	Other:	
	Other:	
	Other:	
	Other:	

VHF Log

Channel	Description	Comment
	Other:	
	Other:	
	Other:	
	Other:	
	Other:	
	Other:	
	Other:	
	Other:	

WINE LOG

Wine Log

Details	Ranking	Comments
Name: Crown Vineyard: Royal Year:	1 ☐ 2 ☐ 3 ☐ 4 ☐ 5 ☐ Order Another Case = 5 Bilge Water = 1	
Name: Vineyard: Year:	1 ☐ 2 ☐ 3 ☐ 4 ☐ 5 ☐	
Name: Vineyard: Year:	1 ☐ 2 ☐ 3 ☐ 4 ☐ 5 ☐	
Name: Vineyard: Year:	1 ☐ 2 ☐ 3 ☐ 4 ☐ 5 ☐	
Name: Vineyard: Year:	1 ☐ 2 ☐ 3 ☐ 4 ☐ 5 ☐	
Name: Vineyard: Year:	1 ☐ 2 ☐ 3 ☐ 4 ☐ 5 ☐	

Wine Log

Details	Ranking	Comments
Name: Vineyard: Year:	1 2 3 4 5 ☐ ☐ ☐ ☐ ☐ Order Another Case = 5 Bilge Water = 1	
Name: Vineyard: Year:	1 2 3 4 5 ☐ ☐ ☐ ☐ ☐	
Name: Vineyard: Year:	1 2 3 4 5 ☐ ☐ ☐ ☐ ☐	
Name: Vineyard: Year:	1 2 3 4 5 ☐ ☐ ☐ ☐ ☐	
Name: Vineyard: Year:	1 2 3 4 5 ☐ ☐ ☐ ☐ ☐	
Name: Vineyard: Year:	1 2 3 4 5 ☐ ☐ ☐ ☐ ☐	

Wine Log

Details	Ranking	Comments
Name: Vineyard: Year:	1 2 3 4 5 ☐ ☐ ☐ ☐ ☐ Wine Spectator Ranking of 95=5 WHINO Spectator Ranking of 95=1	
Name: Vineyard: Year:	1 2 3 4 5 ☐ ☐ ☐ ☐ ☐	
Name: Vineyard: Year:	1 2 3 4 5 ☐ ☐ ☐ ☐ ☐	
Name: Vineyard: Year:	1 2 3 4 5 ☐ ☐ ☐ ☐ ☐	
Name: Vineyard: Year:	1 2 3 4 5 ☐ ☐ ☐ ☐ ☐	
Name: Vineyard: Year:	1 2 3 4 5 ☐ ☐ ☐ ☐ ☐	

Wine Log

Details	Ranking	Comments
Name: Vineyard: Year:	1 2 3 4 5 ☐ ☐ ☐ ☐ ☐ <u>Wine</u> <u>Spectator</u> Ranking of 95=5 <u>WHINO</u> <u>Spectator</u> Ranking of 95=1	
Name: Vineyard: Year:	1 2 3 4 5 ☐ ☐ ☐ ☐ ☐	
Name: Vineyard: Year:	1 2 3 4 5 ☐ ☐ ☐ ☐ ☐	
Name: Vineyard: Year:	1 2 3 4 5 ☐ ☐ ☐ ☐ ☐	
Name: Vineyard: Year:	1 2 3 4 5 ☐ ☐ ☐ ☐ ☐	
Name: Vineyard: Year:	1 2 3 4 5 ☐ ☐ ☐ ☐ ☐	

Wine Log

Details	Ranking	Comments
Name: Vineyard: Year:	1 ☐ 2 ☐ 3 ☐ 4 ☐ 5 ☐ The heck with letting it breath, pour me another = 5 Iraq makes wine? = 1	
Name: Vineyard: Year:	1 ☐ 2 ☐ 3 ☐ 4 ☐ 5 ☐	
Name: Vineyard: Year:	1 ☐ 2 ☐ 3 ☐ 4 ☐ 5 ☐	
Name: Vineyard: Year:	1 ☐ 2 ☐ 3 ☐ 4 ☐ 5 ☐	
Name: Vineyard: Year:	1 ☐ 2 ☐ 3 ☐ 4 ☐ 5 ☐	
Name: Vineyard: Year:	1 ☐ 2 ☐ 3 ☐ 4 ☐ 5 ☐	

Wine Log

Details	Ranking	Comments
Name: Vineyard: Year:	1　2　3　4　5 ☐ ☐ ☐ ☐ ☐ The heck with letting it breath, pour me another = 5 Iraq makes wine? = 1	
Name: Vineyard: Year:	1　2　3　4　5 ☐ ☐ ☐ ☐ ☐	
Name: Vineyard: Year:	1　2　3　4　5 ☐ ☐ ☐ ☐ ☐	
Name: Vineyard: Year:	1　2　3　4　5 ☐ ☐ ☐ ☐ ☐	
Name: Vineyard: Year:	1　2　3　4　5 ☐ ☐ ☐ ☐ ☐	
Name: Vineyard: Year:	1　2　3　4　5 ☐ ☐ ☐ ☐ ☐	

RESTAURANT LOG

Restaurant Log

Date	Details	Ranking	Comments
	Name: Tel #: Location:	1 ☐ 2 ☐ 3 ☐ 4 ☐ 5 ☐ Hello . . . Julia Child!! = 5 Hello . . . Board of Health? = 1	
	Name: Tel #: Location:	1 ☐ 2 ☐ 3 ☐ 4 ☐ 5 ☐	
	Name: Tel #: Location:	1 ☐ 2 ☐ 3 ☐ 4 ☐ 5 ☐	
	Name: Tel #: Location:	1 ☐ 2 ☐ 3 ☐ 4 ☐ 5 ☐	
	Name: Tel #: Location:	1 ☐ 2 ☐ 3 ☐ 4 ☐ 5 ☐	
	Name: Tel #: Location:	1 ☐ 2 ☐ 3 ☐ 4 ☐ 5 ☐	

Restaurant Log

Date	Details	Ranking	Comments
	Name: Tel #: Location:	1 2 3 4 5 ☐ ☐ ☐ ☐ ☐ Hello . . . Julia Child!! = 5 Hello . . . Board of Health? =1	
	Name: Tel #: Location:	1 2 3 4 5 ☐ ☐ ☐ ☐ ☐	
	Name: Tel #: Location:	1 2 3 4 5 ☐ ☐ ☐ ☐ ☐	
	Name: Tel #: Location:	1 2 3 4 5 ☐ ☐ ☐ ☐ ☐	
	Name: Tel #: Location:	1 2 3 4 5 ☐ ☐ ☐ ☐ ☐	
	Name: Tel #: Location:	1 2 3 4 5 ☐ ☐ ☐ ☐ ☐	

Restaurant Log

Date	Details	Ranking	Comments
	Name: Tel #: Location:	1 ☐ 2 ☐ 3 ☐ 4 ☐ 5 ☐ Where's the dessert menu? = 5 Where's the TUMS = 1	
	Name: Tel #: Location:	1 ☐ 2 ☐ 3 ☐ 4 ☐ 5 ☐	
	Name: Tel #: Location:	1 ☐ 2 ☐ 3 ☐ 4 ☐ 5 ☐	
	Name: Tel #: Location:	1 ☐ 2 ☐ 3 ☐ 4 ☐ 5 ☐	
	Name: Tel #: Location:	1 ☐ 2 ☐ 3 ☐ 4 ☐ 5 ☐	
	Name: Tel #: Location:	1 ☐ 2 ☐ 3 ☐ 4 ☐ 5 ☐	

Restaurant Log

Date	Details	Ranking	Comments
	Name: Tel #: Location:	1 ☐ 2 ☐ 3 ☐ 4 ☐ 5 ☐ Where's the dessert menu? = 5 Where's the TUMS = 1	
	Name: Tel #: Location:	1 ☐ 2 ☐ 3 ☐ 4 ☐ 5 ☐	
	Name: Tel #: Location:	1 ☐ 2 ☐ 3 ☐ 4 ☐ 5 ☐	
	Name: Tel #: Location:	1 ☐ 2 ☐ 3 ☐ 4 ☐ 5 ☐	
	Name: Tel #: Location:	1 ☐ 2 ☐ 3 ☐ 4 ☐ 5 ☐	
	Name: Tel #: Location:	1 ☐ 2 ☐ 3 ☐ 4 ☐ 5 ☐	

Restaurant Log

Date	Details	Ranking	Comments
	Name: Tel #: Location:	1 ☐ 2 ☐ 3 ☐ 4 ☐ 5 ☐ Bon Appetite! = 5 Bone in my fish =1	
	Name: Tel #: Location:	1 ☐ 2 ☐ 3 ☐ 4 ☐ 5 ☐	
	Name: Tel #: Location:	1 ☐ 2 ☐ 3 ☐ 4 ☐ 5 ☐	
	Name: Tel #: Location:	1 ☐ 2 ☐ 3 ☐ 4 ☐ 5 ☐	
	Name: Tel #: Location:	1 ☐ 2 ☐ 3 ☐ 4 ☐ 5 ☐	
	Name: Tel #: Location:	1 ☐ 2 ☐ 3 ☐ 4 ☐ 5 ☐	

Restaurant Log

Date	Details	Ranking	Comments
	Name: Tel #: Location:	1 2 3 4 5 ☐ ☐ ☐ ☐ ☐ Bon Appetite! = 5 Bone in my fish = 1	
	Name: Tel #: Location:	1 2 3 4 5 ☐ ☐ ☐ ☐ ☐	
	Name: Tel #: Location:	1 2 3 4 5 ☐ ☐ ☐ ☐ ☐	
	Name: Tel #: Location:	1 2 3 4 5 ☐ ☐ ☐ ☐ ☐	
	Name: Tel #: Location:	1 2 3 4 5 ☐ ☐ ☐ ☐ ☐	
	Name: Tel #: Location:	1 2 3 4 5 ☐ ☐ ☐ ☐ ☐	

WATERING HOLE LOG

"Watering Hole" Log

Date	Details	Ranking	Comments
	Name: Location: "Happy Hour' Starts At: "Ladies Night" Held On:	1 2 3 4 5 ☐ ☐ ☐ ☐ ☐	Why are they serving whiskey out of a plastic jug? =1 (this is bad) Wasn't this place in a Jimmy Buffet song? =5 (this is good)
	Name: Location: "Happy Hour' Starts At: "Ladies Night" Held On:	1 2 3 4 5 ☐ ☐ ☐ ☐ ☐	
	Name: Location: "Happy Hour' Starts At: "Ladies Night" Held On:	1 2 3 4 5 ☐ ☐ ☐ ☐ ☐	
	Name: Location: "Happy Hour' Starts At: "Ladies Night" Held On:	1 2 3 4 5 ☐ ☐ ☐ ☐ ☐	
	Name: Location: "Happy Hour' Starts At: "Ladies Night" Held On:	1 2 3 4 5 ☐ ☐ ☐ ☐ ☐	
	Name: Location: "Happy Hour' Starts At: "Ladies Night" Held On:	1 2 3 4 5 ☐ ☐ ☐ ☐ ☐	

"Watering Hole" Log

Date	Details	Ranking	Comments
	Name: Location: "Happy Hour' Starts At: "Ladies Night" Held On:	1　2　3　4　5 ☐　☐　☐　☐　☐ Why are they serving whiskey out of a plastic jug? =1 (this is bad) Wasn't this place in a Jimmy Buffet song? =5 (this is good)	
	Name: Location: "Happy Hour' Starts At: "Ladies Night" Held On:	1　2　3　4　5 ☐　☐　☐　☐　☐	
	Name: Location: "Happy Hour' Starts At: "Ladies Night" Held On:	1　2　3　4　5 ☐　☐　☐　☐　☐	
	Name: Location: "Happy Hour' Starts At: "Ladies Night" Held On:	1　2　3　4　5 ☐　☐　☐　☐　☐	
	Name: Location: "Happy Hour' Starts At: "Ladies Night" Held On:	1　2　3　4　5 ☐　☐　☐　☐　☐	
	Name: Location: "Happy Hour' Starts At: "Ladies Night" Held On:	1　2　3　4　5 ☐　☐　☐　☐　☐	

"Watering Hole" Log

Date	Details	Ranking	Comments
	Name: Location: "Happy Hour' Starts At: "Ladies Night" Held On:	1 ☐ 2 ☐ 3 ☐ 4 ☐ 5 ☐ There's only Cher and show tunes on the JukeBox =1 (this is bad) There's only Van Morrison on the JukeBox =5 (this is good)	
	Name: Location: "Happy Hour' Starts At: "Ladies Night" Held On:	1 ☐ 2 ☐ 3 ☐ 4 ☐ 5 ☐	
	Name: Location: "Happy Hour' Starts At: "Ladies Night" Held On:	1 ☐ 2 ☐ 3 ☐ 4 ☐ 5 ☐	
	Name: Location: "Happy Hour' Starts At: "Ladies Night" Held On:	1 ☐ 2 ☐ 3 ☐ 4 ☐ 5 ☐	
	Name: Location: "Happy Hour' Starts At: "Ladies Night" Held On:	1 ☐ 2 ☐ 3 ☐ 4 ☐ 5 ☐	
	Name: Location: "Happy Hour' Starts At: "Ladies Night" Held On:	1 ☐ 2 ☐ 3 ☐ 4 ☐ 5 ☐	

"Watering Hole" Log

Date	Details	Ranking	Comments
	Name: Location: "Happy Hour' Starts At: "Ladies Night" Held On:	1 2 3 4 5 ☐ ☐ ☐ ☐ ☐ There's only Cher and show tunes on the JukeBox =1 (this is bad) There's only Van Morrison on the JukeBox =5 (this is good)	
	Name: Location: "Happy Hour' Starts At: "Ladies Night" Held On:	1 2 3 4 5 ☐ ☐ ☐ ☐ ☐	
	Name: Location: "Happy Hour' Starts At: "Ladies Night" Held On:	1 2 3 4 5 ☐ ☐ ☐ ☐ ☐	
	Name: Location: "Happy Hour' Starts At: "Ladies Night" Held On:	1 2 3 4 5 ☐ ☐ ☐ ☐ ☐	
	Name: Location: "Happy Hour' Starts At: "Ladies Night" Held On:	1 2 3 4 5 ☐ ☐ ☐ ☐ ☐	
	Name: Location: "Happy Hour' Starts At: "Ladies Night" Held On:	1 2 3 4 5 ☐ ☐ ☐ ☐ ☐	

MARINA LOG

Marina Log

Details	Comments
Name: Location: Telephone #: Lat: Long: Monitors Channel #'s:	
Name: Location: Telephone #: Lat: Long: Monitors Channel #'s:	
Name: Location: Telephone #: Lat: Long: Monitors Channel #'s:	
Name: Location: Telephone #: Lat: Long: Monitors Channel #'s:	

Marina Log

Details	Comments
Name: Location: Telephone #: Lat: Long: Monitors Channel #'s:	
Name: Location: Telephone #: Lat: Long: Monitors Channel #'s:	
Name: Location: Telephone #: Lat: Long: Monitors Channel #'s:	
Name: Location: Telephone #: Lat: Long: Monitors Channel #'s:	

Marina Log

Details	Comments
Name: Location: Telephone #: Lat: Long: Monitors Channel #'s:	
Name: Location: Telephone #: Lat: Long: Monitors Channel #'s:	
Name: Location: Telephone #: Lat: Long: Monitors Channel #'s:	
Name: Location: Telephone #: Lat: Long: Monitors Channel #'s:	

Marina Log

Details	Comments
Name: Location: Telephone #: Lat: Long: Monitors Channel #'s:	
Name: Location: Telephone #: Lat: Long: Monitors Channel #'s:	
Name: Location: Telephone #: Lat: Long: Monitors Channel #'s:	
Name: Location: Telephone #: Lat: Long: Monitors Channel #'s:	

FISH LOG

Fish Log

Details	Ranking	Comments

Type:
Date/Time:
Location:
 	
Bait/Lure Used:
	Actual Weight/Length:
	    lbs inches
	
	Weight/Length You'll Tell Your Family/Friends:
	    lbs inches	

Type:
Date/Time:
Location:
 	
Bait/Lure Used:
	Actual Weight/Length:
	    lbs inches
	
	Weight/Length You'll Tell Your Family/Friends:
	    lbs inches	

Type:
Date/Time:
Location:
 	
Bait/Lure Used:
	Actual Weight/Length:
	    lbs inches
	
	Weight/Length You'll Tell Your Family/Friends:
	    lbs inches	

Type:
Date/Time:
Location:
 	
Bait/Lure Used:
	Actual Weight/Length:
	    lbs inches
	
	Weight/Length You'll Tell Your Family/Friends:
	    lbs inches	

Fish Log

Details	Ranking	Comments

Type:
Date/Time:
Location:
 	
Bait/Lure Used:
	Actual Weight/Length:
	    lbs inches
	
	Weight/Length You'll Tell Your Family/Friends:
	    lbs inches	

Type:
Date/Time:
Location:
 	
Bait/Lure Used:
	Actual Weight/Length:
	    lbs inches
	
	Weight/Length You'll Tell Your Family/Friends:
	    lbs inches	

Type:
Date/Time:
Location:
 	
Bait/Lure Used:
	Actual Weight/Length:
	    lbs inches
	
	Weight/Length You'll Tell Your Family/Friends:
	    lbs inches	

Type:
Date/Time:
Location:
 	
Bait/Lure Used:
	Actual Weight/Length:
	    lbs inches
	
	Weight/Length You'll Tell Your Family/Friends:
	    lbs inches	

Fish Log

Details	Ranking	Comments

Type:
Date/Time:
Location:
 	
Bait/Lure Used:
	Actual Weight/Length:
	    lbs inches
	
	Weight/Length You'll Tell Your Family/Friends:
	    lbs inches	

Type:
Date/Time:
Location:
 	
Bait/Lure Used:
	Actual Weight/Length:
	    lbs inches
	
	Weight/Length You'll Tell Your Family/Friends:
	    lbs inches	

Type:
Date/Time:
Location:
 	
Bait/Lure Used:
	Actual Weight/Length:
	    lbs inches
	
	Weight/Length You'll Tell Your Family/Friends:
	    lbs inches	

Type:
Date/Time:
Location:
 	
Bait/Lure Used:
	Actual Weight/Length:
	    lbs inches
	
	Weight/Length You'll Tell Your Family/Friends:
	    lbs inches	

Fish Log

Details	Ranking	Comments

Type:
Date/Time:
Location:
 	
Bait/Lure Used:
	Actual Weight/Length:
	    lbs inches
	
	Weight/Length You'll Tell
	Your Family/Friends:
	    lbs inches	

Type:
Date/Time:
Location:
 	
Bait/Lure Used:
	Actual Weight/Length:
	    lbs inches
	
	Weight/Length You'll Tell
	Your Family/Friends:
	    lbs inches	

Type:
Date/Time:
Location:
 	
Bait/Lure Used:
	Actual Weight/Length:
	    lbs inches
	
	Weight/Length You'll Tell
	Your Family/Friends:
	    lbs inches	

Type:
Date/Time:
Location:
 	
Bait/Lure Used:
	Actual Weight/Length:
	    lbs inches
	
	Weight/Length You'll Tell
	Your Family/Friends:
	    lbs inches	

Fish Log

Details	Ranking	Comments

Type:
Date/Time:
Location:
 	
Bait/Lure Used:
	Actual Weight/Length:
	   lbs inches
	
	Weight/Length You'll Tell Your Family/Friends:
	   lbs inches	

Type:
Date/Time:
Location:
 	
Bait/Lure Used:
	Actual Weight/Length:
	   lbs inches
	
	Weight/Length You'll Tell Your Family/Friends:
	   lbs inches	

Type:
Date/Time:
Location:
 	
Bait/Lure Used:
	Actual Weight/Length:
	   lbs inches
	
	Weight/Length You'll Tell Your Family/Friends:
	   lbs inches	

Type:
Date/Time:
Location:
 	
Bait/Lure Used:
	Actual Weight/Length:
	   lbs inches
	
	Weight/Length You'll Tell Your Family/Friends:
	   lbs inches	

Fish Log

Details	Ranking	Comments

Type:
Date/Time:
Location:
 	
Bait/Lure Used:
	Actual Weight/Length:
	    lbs inches
	
	Weight/Length You'll Tell Your Family/Friends:
	    lbs inches	

Type:
Date/Time:
Location:
 	
Bait/Lure Used:
	Actual Weight/Length:
	    lbs inches
	
	Weight/Length You'll Tell Your Family/Friends:
	    lbs inches	

Type:
Date/Time:
Location:
 	
Bait/Lure Used:
	Actual Weight/Length:
	    lbs inches
	
	Weight/Length You'll Tell Your Family/Friends:
	    lbs inches	

Type:
Date/Time:
Location:
 	
Bait/Lure Used:
	Actual Weight/Length:
	    lbs inches
	
	Weight/Length You'll Tell Your Family/Friends:
	    lbs inches	

GPS LOG

GPS LOG

No.	Location	Latitude	Longitude

GPS LOG

No.	Location	Latitude	Longitude

GPS LOG

No.	Location	Latitude	Longitude

GPS LOG

No.	Location	Latitude	Longitude

GPS LOG

No.	Location	Latitude	Longitude

NOTES

Notes

Notes

Notes

Notes

Notes

Notes

Notes

Notes

Notes

Notes

Notes

Notes

CPSIA information can be obtained at www.ICGtesting.com
Printed in the USA
BVOW03*0654090514

352809BV00002B/37/P